HOSEA

GOD'S PERSISTENT LOVE

DALE &
SANDY LARSEN

12 STUDIES
FOR INDIVIDUALS
OR GROUPS

T0324359

Life
Builder
Study

INTER-VARSITY PRESS
36 Causton Street, London SW1P 4ST, England
Email: ivp@ivpbooks.com
Website: www.ivpbooks.com

Originally published in the United States of America in the LifeGuide® Bible Studies series in 1996 by InterVarsity Press, Downers Grove, Illinois
Second edition published 2004
First published in Great Britain by Scripture Union in 1996
Second UK edition published 2015
This edition published in Great Britain by Inter-Varsity Press 2021

British Library Cataloguing-in-Publication Data
A catalogue record for this book is available from the British Library.

ISBN: 978–1–78359–890–8

Printed in Great Britain by Ashford Colour Press Ltd, Gosport, Hampshire

Produced on paper from sustainable sources.

Inter-Varsity Press publishes Christian books that are true to the Bible and that communicate the gospel, develop discipleship and strengthen the church for its mission in the world.

IVP originated within the Inter-Varsity Fellowship, now the Universities and Colleges Christian Fellowship, a student movement connecting Christian Unions in universities and colleges throughout Great Britain, and a member movement of the International Fellowship of Evangelical Students. Website: www.uccf.org.uk. That historic association is maintained, and all senior IVP staff and committee members subscribe to the UCCF Basis of Faith.

Contents

Getting the Most Out of *Hosea*

In choosing to study Hosea you have ventured into a turbulent place of love and justice, promise and pain, close to the heart of God. You are also in scriptural territory unfamiliar to many Christians.

Even dedicated Bible readers often skip the Minor Prophets, the twelve short books crowded at the end of the Old Testament. The word *minor* makes them sound unimportant, although it means only that they are the shortest books of prophecy. They are sprinkled with strange geographical and historical references. But their power and emotion grab us as soon as we look into the first of the Minor Prophets: the book of Hosea.

The prophecy of Hosea does not progress logically from beginning to conclusion. Its writing is circular, going back and forth between judgment and mercy. We get a sense of God arguing with himself about Israel—not that God has trouble deciding what to do, but he feels the pain of conflict between what he *wants* for Israel and what he *must do* because of their sin.

Hosea shares God's conflict when at God's command he marries—and stays married to—the immoral woman Gomer. It is the conflict of anyone who cares deeply about a wayward person. God condemns Israel's sin and knows Israel deserves to be written off; yet he hangs on, unwilling to give up on them. God eventually let Israel be defeated in the Assyrian conquest, but he did not ultimately abandon his people whom he loved.

Setting the Stage

Hosea's prophecies begin during the forty-one-year reign of Jeroboam II in the eighth century B.C. Jeroboam's rule, militarily successful but religiously corrupt, is concisely described in 2 Kings 14:23-29. He was a military success but a spiritual failure.

Though Jeroboam is the only king of Israel mentioned by name in Hosea (1:1), the list of the kings of Judah show that Hosea's prophetic ministry extended over a fifty-year period and may encompass the conquest of Israel by Assyria in 722 B.C. The reigns of the four Judean kings are described in 2 Chronicles 26:1—32:33. It was a time of prosperity, with Israel and Judah controlling the international trade route. But it was also a time of idolatry and corruption as the Israelites, seeking success and security, adopted practices of the surrounding pagan cultures.

In pagan agrarian society, the accepted way to assure good harvests was through ritual worship of fertility gods, the Baals and Asherahs condemned in the Old Testament. Israel observed the practice, liked the promised results and enthusiastically entered into pagan worship. No doubt they did not consider that they had abandoned God. They were simply employing the latest "technology" to achieve the best possible harvest.

As the Israelites asserted more control over their destiny and trusted God less, they also began to manipulate one another. Injustice became the rule of life. In chasing a better life, Israel cut themselves off from their moral roots that reached back to Moses and the Ten Commandments and further back to Abraham.

The absence of moral roots is clear in the chaos of Israel's monarchy after the death of Jeroboam II, when king after king was assassinated (2 Kings 15:8-31). No doubt most of Hosea's prophecies were given during this time. While Hosea wrote about the unfaithfulness of Israel, Amos, his contemporary, painted a picture of their self-indulgence: "You lie on beds inlaid with ivory and lounge on your couches. You dine on choice lambs and fattened calves. You strum on your harps like David and improvise on musical instruments. You drink wine by the bowlful and use the finest lotions, but you do not grieve over the ruin of Joseph" (Amos 6:4-6).

Adultery and prostitution are the ugly pictures Hosea used to describe Israel's spiritual condition. The image of sexual immorality not only symbolized Israel's running after other gods and turning to other nations for protection, it also literally described their acts with temple prostitutes that were part of the fertility rites they had adopted. Hosea grieved over a nation once pledged to God but now unfaithful.

What could God do with these people whom he loved but whose sins he hated? That was the question that faced God in the time of Hosea. It is the question we ask ourselves when we love someone who is wandering morally. It's also the question God asks about us when, through our sin, we are unfaithful to him.

May God bring you even closer to his heart as you study the book of Hosea.

Suggestions for Individual Study

1. As you begin each study, pray that God will speak to you through his Word.

2. Read the introduction to the study and respond to the personal reflection question or exercise. This is designed to help you focus on God and on the theme of the study.

3. Each study deals with a particular passage—so that you can delve into the author's meaning in that context. Read and reread the passage to be studied. The questions are written using the language of the New International Version, so you may wish to use that version of the Bible. The New Revised Standard Version is also recommended.

4. This is an inductive Bible study, designed to help you discover for yourself what Scripture is saying. The study includes three types of questions. *Observation* questions ask about the basic facts: who, what, when, where and how. *Interpretation* questions delve into the meaning of the passage. *Application* questions help you discover the implications of the text for growing in Christ. These three keys unlock the treasures of Scripture.

Write your answers to the questions in the spaces provided or in a personal journal. Writing can bring clarity and deeper understanding of yourself and of God's Word.

5. It might be good to have a Bible dictionary handy. Use it to look up any unfamiliar words, names or places.

6. Use the prayer suggestion to guide you in thanking God for what you have learned and to pray about the applications that have come to mind.

7. You may want to go on to the suggestion under "Now or Later," or you may want to use that idea for your next study.

Suggestions for Members of a Group Study

1. Come to the study prepared. Follow the suggestions for individual study mentioned above. You will find that careful preparation will greatly enrich your time spent in group discussion.

2. Be willing to participate in the discussion. The leader of your group will not be lecturing. Instead, he or she will be encouraging the members of the group to discuss what they have learned. The leader will be asking the questions that are found in this guide.

3. Stick to the topic being discussed. Your answers should be based on the verses which are the focus of the discussion and not on outside authorities such as commentaries or speakers. These studies focus on a particular passage of Scripture. Only rarely should you refer to other portions of the Bible. This allows for everyone to participate in in-depth study on equal ground.

4. Be sensitive to the other members of the group. Listen attentively when they describe what they have learned. You may be surprised by their insights! Each question assumes a variety of answers. Many questions do not have "right" answers, particularly questions that aim at meaning or application. Instead the questions push us to explore the passage more thoroughly.

When possible, link what you say to the comments of others. Also, be affirming whenever you can. This will encourage some of the more hesitant members of the group to participate.

5. Be careful not to dominate the discussion. We are sometimes so eager to express our thoughts that we leave too little opportunity for others to respond. By all means participate! But allow others to also.

6. Expect God to teach you through the passage being discussed and through the other members of the group. Pray that you will have an enjoyable and profitable time together, but also that as a result of the study you will find ways that you can take action individually and/or as a group.

7. Remember that anything said in the group is considered confidential and should not be discussed outside the group unless specific permission is given to do so.

8. If you are the group leader, you will find additional suggestions at the back of the guide.

1

A Share in God's Pain

We returned from a year overseas to find four couples we knew in the process of divorce. The relationships had once been full of hope and promise. What had gone wrong? Their stories differed, but all were full of pain, not only for the partners but also for everyone who cared about them. Pain among people who love each other—or once loved each other—is common to humanity.

GROUP DISCUSSION. Think of a time someone asked you to do something so difficult that you responded, "Not me!" Did you later reconsider? What made you change your mind? If you didn't do that thing, do you now wish you had? Why?

PERSONAL REFLECTION. What is the most difficult thing anyone has ever asked you to do? Prayerfully reflect on your choice and the outcome.

Hosea proclaimed God's message to the Jewish people in the eighth century B.C. It was a time of prosperity and success mixed with spiritual corruption and idolatry. We do not know how Hosea became a prophet except that "the word of the LORD" came to him (1:1). Hosea grieved over a people once pledged to God but now unfaithful. *Read Hosea 1:1—2:1.*

1. What unusually difficult commands did God give Hosea, and how did he respond?

2. If you had been Hosea, at what point would you have dropped out and told God you would not cooperate with his plan? Or do you believe you would have carried through to the end, and why?

3. While she was married to Hosea but unfaithful to him, Gomer gave birth to three children (1:3, 6, 8). What mixed feelings would Hosea have had about the children?

4. The Lord explained that Hosea's marriage to Gomer would symbolize God's relationship with unfaithful Israel (1:2). How does marriage to an adulterous spouse illustrate God's relationship with sinful humanity?

5. Christians often say that we are called to "hate the sin but love the sinner." What conflicts arise when a person intends to be both just and merciful?

6. In this passage how does God proclaim to Israel both his justice and his mercy?

7. *Read Hosea 2:2-13.* How would you describe the moods and emotions you detect in God's words about Israel?

8. What were God's purposes in persistently punishing Israel (2:6-10)?

9. What would Israel lose because they had rebelled (2:9-13)?

10. When have you, like Hosea, had a close relationship with a person who was rebelling against God? Describe how this feels.

11. What does this passage reveal to you about how your own sin affects the Lord?

Thank God for his justice and his mercy. Pray privately for one person who needs to face up to sin and come to know the forgiving love of God. Ask the Lord to love that person through you.

Now or Later

Consider this question: Why is spiritual growth more likely to result from obeying God in hard things rather than easy things? Discuss your reasons with someone, make journal entries or both.

2

A Vision of
the Possible

The first step. The first alphabet printed with crayon. The first time behind the steering wheel. The first job. Those joyful "firsts" thrill us not so much for themselves as for their promise that this child will mature into a strong, capable person, one for whom walking and writing and driving and working are normal parts of life. Each of us wants to see the people we love fulfill their highest potential.

GROUP DISCUSSION. Tell about someone who had a dream for you and encouraged you to do your best and even beyond your best.

PERSONAL REFLECTION. Who comes to your mind when you see the word *encourager*? What difference has that person made in your life?

Our dreams can be self-centered, such as when we long for another person to carry out our own frustrated plans. God has a vision for his people, and his vision is pure, healthy and wholly for their own good. We have seen how sin has broken the heart of Hosea and of the Lord. Now God offers a fuller vision of the hope he held out in 1:10-11. *Read Hosea 2:14-23.*

1. In your own words, sum up God's vision for his people's future as it is stated through Hosea's poetic language.

2. In contrast to the first part of chapter 2, this passage offers hope for Israel. How does God's forgiveness give you hope?

3. What changes did the Lord want to see his people make in response to his love?

4. What indications do you see that God would take steps to bring reconciliation between himself and Israel?

5. In 2:22-23 the Lord refers to the names of Gomer's three children (see 1:4-8). What has now changed?

6. *Read Hosea 3:1-5.* In addition to the difficult commands of chapter 1, what did God now ask Hosea to do?

7. Put yourself in Hosea's place. How do you think you would have responded to God's command?

8. Besides the money and grain (3:2), what else would Hosea have to give up to get Gomer back?

9. In 2:15 God said he would make the Valley of Achor ("trouble") "a door of hope." Israel knew Achor as a valley of defeat where Achan sinned by keeping part of the Jericho plunder (Joshua 7). What place, event or situation is a "Valley of Achor" for you—a place of spiritual defeat?

10. What would it mean for God to turn your "Valley of Achor" into a "door of hope"?

What steps of obedience and trust do you need to take in order to realize that hope?

Thank the Lord for the hope you have because of his mercy.

Now or Later

Draw a house with a shaky foundation of crumbling stones. Label each broken stone with a popular but false hope in which people commonly put their trust. Circle the stones that represent false hopes that still attract you. Draw another house with a solid foundation. Label its stones with trustworthy hopes such as God's love, God's forgiveness, heaven and the presence of the Holy Spirit.

3

Back to the Present

When we arrived to teach English in Kharkov, Ukraine, two students took us sightseeing. Oleg proudly showed off the beauties of his city. Slava followed behind, bad-mouthing every building and monument, saying how terrible life was since the fall of communism. Finally we asked, "Slava, are you a pessimist?"

"No," he answered, "I am a realist."

Slava turned out to be a pessimist above all pessimists but a great friend too. On the other hand, a person who is upbeat about *everything* becomes tiresome, then irritating. The time comes when we have to admit how bad some things really are.

GROUP DISCUSSION. Do you feel hopeful or discouraged about our society, and why?

PERSONAL REFLECTION. What have you read in or heard on the news lately that has given you hope? What have you read or heard that has discouraged you?

Immediately after the vision of reconciliation in chapter 3, the Lord led Hosea to prophesy about the terrible consequences of Israel's sin. *Read Hosea 4.*

1. What generalizations can you make about Israelite society in Hosea's time?

2. How close is Hosea's description to the state of your own society?

3. Although many sins are mentioned in this passage, which one does God repeatedly condemn (see especially vv. 10-14)?

4. Why is prostitution an apt symbol of worshiping false gods (besides a literal part of Baal worship)?

5. What light does this shed on God's command to Hosea in 1:2?

6. Christians are sometimes accused of "selling out" the gospel of Christ. What examples of this accusation have you heard?

7. What sort of gain tempts you to compromise your loyalty to Christ?

8. Why does God choose to show mercy to the "daughters" and "daughters-in-law" (v. 14)?

9. How does this passage answer a person who says, "It doesn't matter what you worship as long as you have something to believe in"?

10. What does verse 16 tell you about the heart of God?

11. Hosea 4 reveals that Israel was in a sad state in Hosea's time. If you had lived then, how well would you have fit in with Israelite society? Would you have blended in and gone with the drift, or would you have dared to be different? Why do you answer as you do?

12. To what extent do you think you go along with sin in your own society?

13. Where do you need to change in order to stand out as a worshiper of the Lord?

Pray that you will live in faithfulness, love and acknowledgment of God no matter whether your society approves or not (see v. 1).

Now or Later

Since "sins of the leadership" is the subject of study 4, reread Hosea 4:6-9 in light of the particular sins of the Jewish priests. Consider these questions:

• How had the priests failed the people?

• Why do you think God held the people responsible even though the priests had misled them (v. 9)?

4

Sins of
the Leadership

Hosea 5

Only days after he performed a wedding, a minister confessed to a long-standing extramarital affair. When the new bride heard about it, she wept with disappointment and anger. "How could he stand up there and say all those beautiful things about marriage?" she demanded. Who could answer her?

GROUP DISCUSSION. When a leader (whether religious or secular) falls morally, are you more disappointed than when an "ordinary" person falls? Why or why not?

PERSONAL REFLECTION. Think of a time you were let down by a leader (whether religious or secular). Were you more disappointed than if an "ordinary" person had let you down? Why or why not?

In Hosea 4, God issued strong words of judgment against the idolatry of the Israelites in general. Then he got more specific about the sins of particular classes of people. *Read Hosea 5.*

1. What values had replaced love for the Lord in the hearts of Israel's leaders?

2. So far in Hosea we have read some of the sternest words of judgment anyone could imagine. Yet God continued to speak severely through Hosea. What do you think God was trying to accomplish with so much repetition?

3. Verse 1 says that the leaders have been "a snare" and "a net." Consider recent news, both national and international. How have bad leaders trapped the common people?

4. Israel made some attempts to seek the Lord (vv. 4-7). Why were their attempts not successful?

5. Today many people show an increased spiritual interest, but often their interest is in a non-Christian direction. What may keep people who are interested in spirituality from connecting with the God of the Bible?

6. What further warnings did God give to Israel and Judah in verses 8-12?

7. In the middle of his words of judgment, God said, "I proclaim what is certain" (v. 9). What difference would it make if God's judgment were *not* certain?

8. Where did Israel go to try to find a substitute for God's help (v. 13)?

9. Where do many of today's leaders turn for powerful help as a substitute for God?

10. Think about a leadership position you hold. It may involve a small sphere of influence or may be quite large. When have you been tempted to "turn to Assyria" for help rather than turning to the Lord?

11. What comfort do you take from the concluding words of chapter 5?

Thank God for leaders who are faithful to him. Pray that the Lord will give you godly leaders in your church, your community and your nation. Pray that you will rely on him in any leadership position you hold.

Now or Later

Identify some present-day leaders who show godly character. They may be local, regional or national, religious or secular. Write a note of appreciation to one of them. Express your respect and gratitude for that person's leadership. Mention specific examples or reasons. (You do not have to agree with all of the leader's policies in order to recognize the person's consistent moral character.)

5

A Temporary Repentance

A little boy spilled juice on a white rug. It was an accident; he was sorry; all was forgiven. Not long afterward he took a glass of red Kool-Aid straight to the same rug, got his mother's attention, grinned at her and poured the red stuff directly on the rug. This time Mom was not so lenient!

When we do wrong, it's easy to say "Oops!" or "I guess I slipped up." It takes a deeper level of honesty and commitment to say "I'm sorry," mean it and to resolve not to repeat the action.

GROUP DISCUSSION. How do you judge whether someone is sincere when he or she says "I'm sorry"?

PERSONAL REFLECTION. When someone apologizes to you, do you forgive right away, or do you wait until the person shows evidence that he or she is sorry? Why?

Through the first five chapters of Hosea we have seen the rebellion of God's people. The next part of the book begins with a refreshing change. *Read Hosea 6:1-10.*

1. What happens in this passage that you have not seen so far in Hosea?

2. What did Israel hope to receive from the Lord if they returned to him (vv. 1-3)?

3. Why was the Lord unsatisfied with their supposed repentance (vv. 4-6)?

4. When have you dealt with a person who apologized to you but apparently for selfish motives? What happened long-term?

5. How does the Lord identify the evidence of true repentance (v. 6)?

6. Most of Exodus, Leviticus, Numbers and Deuteronomy are given over to the law of God, with much attention on proper worship and various sacrifices and offerings. Scripture makes it plain that God gave those laws; they were not human inventions. Then what do you think God means when he announces, "I desire mercy, not sacrifice, and acknowledgment of God rather than burnt offerings" (v. 6)?

7. Why is such evidence more trustworthy than the performance of ritual sacrifices?

8. What sort of behavior betrayed Israel's supposed repentance (vv. 7-10)?

9. Our motives for returning to God will never be one hundred percent pure, but the Lord does draw a line here between sincere and insincere repentance. In what areas of your life do you tend to make a superficial repentance?

10. Why do you think you get stuck at a halfway point to full repentance?

In that area of your life, what would true repentance mean for you? (What would it look like? What changes would you make?)

Thank God for the mercy he shows you and for the mercy other people have shown you. Pray that your life will show a spirit of mercy.

Now or Later

Write a letter to the Lord to express more thorough and more personal responses to questions 9 and 10. As a fuller answer to question 10, draw a literal picture or a word picture of the changes you want to make with God's help.

6

No Place to Hide

Hosea 6:11—7:16

Remember playing hide-and-seek? While the person who was "it" counted to one hundred, you ran and found a place to hide. No matter how well you concealed yourself, you held your breath when "it" sang out, "Ready or not, here I come!" Were you really as well hidden as you hoped? Or would you have to sheepishly come out of hiding because "it" found you right away?

God does not have to play hide-and-seek to find out where we are. He sees us all the time and knows us inside and out. "Nothing in all creation is hidden from God's sight. Everything is uncovered and laid bare before the eyes of him to whom we must give account" (Hebrews 4:13).

GROUP DISCUSSION. As a child (or maybe even as an adult), were you ever warned: "God sees everything you do"? If so, what effect did it have on you?

PERSONAL REFLECTION. Think about the fact that God sees everything you do. Is the idea comforting or unsettling? Why?

Mirrors tell the truth, but we can lie to ourselves about what the mirror tells us. God tried to tell the Israelites that their character was sliding downhill. They preferred to believe the best about themselves. *Read Hosea 6:11—7:16.*

1. Throughout this passage, notice the things to which God compares Israel (7:4-8, 11-12, 16). What element of Israel's character does each comparison point out?

2. How might one of those comparisons apply to you?

3. How did Israel (also called Samaria and Ephraim) imagine they were fooling God (7:1-2)?

4. How were they actually deceiving themselves (7:2, 9-10, 14)?

5. Why does deceit lead to destruction (7:13)?

6. What sometimes makes a lie more attractive than the truth?

7. In spite of everything, what did the Lord continue to desire to do for Israel (7:1, 13, 15)?

8. What does God's persistence tell you about his love?

9. "God sees everything you do" is sometimes used as a warning to make children behave. As adults we may hear it as childish or manipulative. Yet this is the message of Hosea 7, and it does not come across as infantile. How would you state the great truth of God's omniscience to someone who needs to hear and believe it?

10. What are some ways that people today imagine they can get away with things God does not see?

11. In what area(s) of your life do you need to remember that you can't deceive or hide from God?

12. How will you plan to live more transparently before God this week?

Thank the Lord that he is always honest with you. Pray for the courage to abandon all deception toward God, yourself and one another.

Now or Later

God used comparisons (metaphors and similes) to show the Israelites how they had wandered from him and to try to turn them back to himself. An example of a metaphor is Hosea 7:8: "Ephraim *is* a flat cake not turned over" (emphasis ours). An example of a simile is Hosea 7:11: "Ephraim *is like* a dove" or Hosea 7:16: "They *are like* a faulty bow" (emphasis ours).

Draw some comparisons to describe your own spiritual life and your relationship with God. Use this pattern:

"I used to be . . . "   "Now I am . . ."   "I hope to become . . ."
"I used to be like . . ." "Now I am like . . ." "I hope to become like . . ."

Examples:

I used to be a wilted flower. Now I am a newly sprouted seed. I hope to become a towering oak.

I used to be like a junk car. Now I am like a minivan that needs a tune-up. I hope to become like an Indy 500 race car.

7

Substitute Gods

We naturally want the best out of life: prosperity, health, security and enjoyment. In his book *Idols of Our Time*, Bob Goudzwaard warns that sooner or later such goals turn into gods on which we become dependent. "Because people put themselves in a position of dependence on their gods, invariably the moment comes when those things or forces gain the upper hand."* It takes courage for us to identify and admit our own idols.

GROUP DISCUSSION. How would you define the good life? How will you know (or how do you know) when you have achieved it?

PERSONAL REFLECTION. When have you trusted in something that you later realized was an idol? How did God show you that the idol had replaced him in your heart? What happened when you saw the truth?

Though Israel claimed to "acknowledge" or "know" God, God did not accept their self-congratulatory claims. *Read Hosea 8.*

---

1. What evidence did the Lord offer that Israel did not really acknowledge him as Lord?

2. Do you think you can tell if people are worshiping sincerely or insincerely? How?

3. Even though Israel worshiped other gods, why did they feel confident that they were still good Israelites, committed to God (8:11-13)?

4. What would be the tragic results of Israel's insincerity (8:7, 10, 13-14)?

5. What are some common idols people today trust in instead of God?

6. Which ones are (or have been) particularly attractive to you?

7. *Read Hosea 9:1-9.* Apparently this passage describes a harvest festival. What warning does God give to Israel concerning their harvest?

8. What would eventually happen to Israel's sacrifices, and why (9:1-4)?

9. What part does God play in your view of what it means to prosper?

10. Describe the contrast between how God viewed the prophet and how the people viewed the prophet (9:7-8).

11. Where do you detect the same scornful attitude toward God's messengers today?

12. In order to be more prosperous, Israel abandoned their role as God's special people and adopted the ways of the nations around them. What guidelines help you evaluate the ways of the world to decide where you can participate and where you would be drawn toward idolatry?

13. Where do you need to have stricter guidelines to steer away from idolatry and keep God first in your life?

Thank the Lord for the good life he has given you. Pray for wisdom to discern false gods that would rob you of your God-given blessings.

Now or Later

Write out your goals for this week, this year and five years from now. (Choose other lengths of time if you prefer and as they fit your circumstances.)

Circle goals that you feel confident the Lord approves of and is with you on.

Draw a rectangle around goals that are not so clearly in accordance with what God wants for you.

Put a question mark next to goals that you think you need to modify to bring them in line with God's will as you discern it.

Put an X by goals that you will put on hold until the Lord shows you whether or not you should pursue them.

*Bob Goudzwaard, *Idols of Our Time,* trans. Mark Vander Vennen (Downers Grove, Ill.: InterVarsity Press, 1984), p. 13.

8

Recalling
Young Love

The Russian Orthodox wedding in the cavernous cathedral clearly followed ancient tradition. The gold-robed priest droned his endless chant, incense filled the air, attendants held crowns over the heads of the bride and groom. There was one jarring anachronism: a person in casual dress videotaped the ceremony from all angles.

Why do people videotape their weddings or pay a small fortune for a wedding photographer? They never want to forget the day they began their life together. It's an event and a pledge to which they can return in times of doubt or conflict.

GROUP DISCUSSION. What are some highlights of your Christian experience? What helps you remember those times?

PERSONAL REFLECTION. What keepsakes or mementos remind you of God's grace toward you?

Could God be disappointed? In this passage from Hosea, God's joy when he began his connection with Israel turns to bitterness when they do not yield the spiritual fruit he desires. *Read Hosea 9:10-17.*

1. Over the years, how had Israel's relationship with God changed?

2. Why are the "fruit" images appropriate for the changing relationship between God and Israel (9:10, 16)?

3. When have you experienced times of dullness or sourness in your relationship with the Lord? How do you explain them (if you can)?

4. Besides the unfruitful vine, what other images of barrenness fill these verses (9:11-14, 16)?

5. *Read Hosea 10:1-15.* Notice how the vine image continues in verse 1. Because they had abandoned their early love for the Lord, what did Hosea predict for Israel's future (10:2-8)?

6. How do you think abandonment of God has affected your own culture?

7. How does God's purpose for Israel contrast with the way they lived (10:9-13)?

8. What did God challenge Israel to do and with what promise (10:12)?

9. How would you like to see your society take up the challenge and receive the fruit of verse 12?

10. What would it mean for you to personally take up the challenge of 10:12?

11. What particular failing led to Israel's harvest of evil (10:13-15)?

12. In what areas do you think you have lost some of the vitality of your first love for the Lord?

13. What new choices (or renewal of former choices) will you make in order to purify your loyalty and restore your first love for God?

Pray for freshness and renewal of your love for God. Thank him that he has never abandoned his love for you.

Now or Later

In Hosea 10:12, God told Israel:

Sow for yourselves righteousness,
  reap the fruit of unfailing love,
and break up your unplowed ground;
  for it is time to seek the LORD,
until he comes
  and showers righteousness on you.

Think of an area of your life where you tend to keep God out or at least do not let him have the last word. Or perhaps it is an area where you have never considered that God has a part or is interested. Draw a flat, unplowed field to represent that area of your life, which is your "unplowed ground" to be broken up.

"Seek the Lord." Pray about what it would mean for you to invite him fully into that area of your life. Draw lines to represent furrows that you are plowing in the field.

(From this point the drawings will not be to scale.) In the middle of the field, draw yourself as a sower with a shoulder bag for seeds.

Draw and label some "seeds" that would go into the bag. The seeds are actions which you will do in order to "sow righteousness" in the field of that part of your life.

Pray that the Lord "showers righteousness on you." Make a commitment to pray that you will "reap the fruit of unfailing love" in that newly plowed and planted part of your life. Stay on the alert for the results God brings.

9

Mercy Overrules

Hosea 11:1-11

You get into your car in the church parking lot and you're about to start the engine when you feel a jolt and hear a metallic crunch. Somebody has backed into you. You jump out, furious, ready to tell off the other driver. Then you see that it's the teenage daughter of a good friend. She gets out of her car but is too stricken and guilty to say much of anything. You know it must be her first car accident. Though you're still upset and your fender is still crumpled, mercy melts your heart. "It's okay, we'll work it out," you say, then give her a hug.

GROUP DISCUSSION. What is the difference between being merciful and being wishy-washy?

PERSONAL REFLECTION. When has someone showed you mercy? How has it made a difference in your life?

For centuries God had continued faithful to Israel, but they spurned his faithfulness and preferred other gods. *Read Hosea 11:1-11.*

1. What emotions do you sense in this passage?

2. What does this passage tell you about the heart of God?

3. In what ways does this passage characterize your own history with the Lord?

4. Centuries before Hosea, Israel followed God out of Egypt in the exodus (v. 1). How does God describe his care for the Israelites during that time (vv. 1-4)?

5. What had the nation of Israel forgotten (or neglected) both at that time and in the intervening years (vv. 2-3, 7)?

6. As the Lord stated repeatedly through Hosea, what would be the consequences of Israel's rebellion (vv. 5-7)?

7. Even in the midst of righteous anger, what pain and longing did God express (vv. 8-9)?

8. Think of occasions when you want to blow up at somebody, but then you change your mind. What makes you back off?

9. In verse 9 the Lord states that "I am God, and not man." It seems elementary to state that God is not a man. What are the deeper implications of the statement?

—————————————————————————————

10. What assurance do you draw from the fact that "I am God, and not man"?

—————————————————————————————

11. How would God demonstrate his mercy to Israel (vv. 10-11)?

—————————————————————————————

12. In what way do you need to offer someone your mercy (and through you, the mercy of God)?

Thank the Lord that he is merciful. Thank him specifically for his mercy toward you. Ask him to help you extend mercy to others.

Now or Later

The heart of God longs for you just as he longed for the Israelites in Hosea's time. Choose a symbol of the Lord's mercy: a small cross, a nail, a stone (for the stone rolled over the door of Christ's tomb) or some memento of an event in which you experienced God's mercy. Place the object where you will see it often. In times of discouragement or rebellion, let it remind you that God loves you and gave his Son to forgive your sins. If you are also burdened for a wandering family member or friend, let the object remind you that God's heart also longs after that person.

10

Yet Justice Prevails

Hosea 11:12—12:14

When mass murderer Jeffrey Dahmer was killed in prison, people were shocked that authorities had not protected him from his enemies. At the same time, most people felt that he got what he deserved. Justice had been done.

Everyone has an inborn sense of justice. We think things ought to work out fairly, though we know they often don't. Much as we like mercy, we get impatient when we see too much of it. Shouldn't justice be satisfied too?

GROUP DISCUSSION. Why does knowing someone's history help you understand the person's present behavior?

PERSONAL REFLECTION. When has your attitude toward someone improved because you found out something about that person's history? What made the difference?

Jacob, son of Isaac and grandson of Abraham, was the first person to be named Israel (Genesis 32:28). *Read Hosea 11:12—12:14.*

---

1. What aspects of Jacob's up-and-down career does this passage recount?

2. Since the historical Jacob was long dead, why do you think certain events from his life are told here?

---

3. Based on what you know of Jacob, how does your spiritual history resemble his (see especially 12:1-4, 12)?

---

4. The heart of the preceding study was the mercy of God. However, if we focus solely on God's mercy, we do not see the whole story. What does this passage reveal about other truths of God's character?

---

5. At first glance, love and justice appear to be mutually exclusive: we can practice one or the other but not both at once. Yet in verse 12:6, God tells Israel to maintain both love and justice. What would be an example of both in action at once?

---

6. What did Israel boast about (12:7-8)?

---

7. Why was their boasting self-deceptive?

---

8. What are some areas of life where you are tempted to brag?

9. How did Hosea continue to use Israel's history to warn them of God's impending judgment (12:9-14)?

10. How does your own spiritual history give you respect for God's justice?

11. Where, or with whom, do you need to be more just, without sacrificing love?

Pray for wisdom to discern the just and right thing to do. Thank God that he is just.

Now or Later

Consider specific ways to put into practice each of the commands from Hosea 12:6: Return to your God, maintain love and justice, and wait for your God always. Write out prayers to the Lord about each of those three commitments (no doubt they will overlap). Resolve to read the prayers again at least weekly.

11

The Sign of Love

"I'm doing this for your own good." "This hurts me more than it hurts you." As children we had trouble believing those words. Now we realize that balanced discipline is evidence of love. Even a puppy wants to know the rules and is more secure when its master clearly enforces the lines of discipline.

GROUP DISCUSSION. Recall a time from your childhood when you were disciplined fairly and with love. How did the discipline help you? What did it teach you about yourself and about the person who disciplined you?

PERSONAL REFLECTION. Is there someone you often feel both affection and anger toward? How do you sort out your feelings in order to be merciful and just toward that person?

God's chosen people were rescued from slavery, given a special revelation of his law, and miraculously brought into a land of milk and honey! What better beginning could a nation have? Sadly, Israel chose to forget what God had done for them. *Read Hosea 13.*

1. Trace the stages of Israel's spiritual decline in this chapter.

2. Where do you discern warnings for yourself in this passage?

3. Verse 1 says that Israel fell into Baal worship and "died." They did not physically die as a nation; in fact, verse 2 says that they continued to increase in idolatry. Then in what sense did their idol worship result in death?

4. Through Hosea, the Lord used powerful images to express the consequences of Israel's idolatry (vv. 3, 7-8). What do the images of Israel's destiny (v. 3) have in common?

5. What elements are shared by the images of what God will do to Israel (vv. 7-8)?

6. In spite of Israel's idolatry and other sins, what purpose does the Lord still hold for them (v. 4)?

7. How does God's purpose for his people explain the severity of his judgment throughout this passage (and all of the book of Hosea)?

8. What encouragement do you gain from God's continuing purpose for his people, including yourself?

9. Verse 9 is a particularly tragic declaration of the reason for Israel's decline. Why would a nation—or a person—turn against the divine Helper?

10. In the midst of his words of judgment, the Lord made a majestic promise of redemption from death (v. 14). Paul quoted this verse in 1 Corinthians 15:55 (altered slightly because Paul quoted from the Greek version of the Old Testament). This promise has inspired hope at countless Christian funerals and has found its way into Handel's *Messiah*. What qualities of the Lord make his promise possible?

11. When has God's loving discipline brought you back to him?

12. Where do you believe God is disciplining you right now, and what will you do to yield to his discipline?

Praise God for his love that will not let you go. Thank him for his discipline, which is evidence that he loves you.

Now or Later

Study Hebrews 12:4-13, the great New Testament statement of why God disciplines his children.

12

God's Final Promise

"Cross my heart and hope to die, stick a needle in my eye." With those words we confirmed the promises of childhood. Of course there was always an "out." The promises didn't count if we crossed our fingers behind our back!

"Sure, I'll be there." "Count on me to help." "You can borrow my car anytime." The words mean nothing if the promiser doesn't produce. We'd rather hear no promise at all than be a victim of a broken promise.

GROUP DISCUSSION. Think of someone who unfailingly keeps his or her promises. How is the person regarded by others? How does dependability show up in other aspects of the person's life?

PERSONAL REFLECTION. Do you have trouble keeping promises? Why (or why not)?

In the final chapter of any book, we expect the author to tie up loose ends and reprise the book's main themes. The prophet Hosea does not disappoint us. *Read Hosea 14.*

1. How does the mood of this passage differ from the other passages of Hosea you read during this study?

2. The Lord urged Israel to "take words with you and return to the LORD" (v. 2). Express in your own words what God longed to hear Israel say (vv. 2-3).

3. Sometimes sincere repentance from the heart is the most difficult offering to make to God. What substitutes do you sometimes bring to the Lord in the place of honest words of repentance?

4. What does the Lord commit himself to do for Israel (vv. 4-8)?

5. How would you characterize the future that God promises for his people (vv. 4-8)?

6. How have you experienced "rooting" and "flourishing" under God's faithful care?

7. What conditions must Israel meet in order to be part of this future with the Lord (see especially vv. 1-3, 9)?

8. Why wouldn't the Lord just say, "Don't worry about your idol worship; we'll overlook that"?

---

9. How have your ideas about God been changed by your study of Hosea?

---

10. How have your ideas about God been confirmed by your study of Hosea?

---

11. With what "words" do you need to "return to the Lord" now?

As your prayer, write or speak your response to question 11.

Now or Later

Study some of the promises of God in both the Old Testament and New Testament. Note the promises that God has kept for you, and offer him praise for his faithfulness.

Take to heart any promises of God that you especially need right now. Memorize them and write them where you will see them regularly. (Carefully read the context of the Scripture passage to be sure that the promise applies to all believers and is not specific for one person or one group for one time.)

Leader's Notes

MY GRACE IS SUFFICIENT FOR YOU. (2 COR 12:9)

Leading a Bible discussion can be an enjoyable and rewarding experience. But it can also be *scary*—especially if you've never done it before. If this is your feeling, you're in good company. When God asked Moses to lead the Israelites out of Egypt, he replied, "O Lord, please send someone else to do it!" (Ex 4:13). It was the same with Solomon, Jeremiah and Timothy, but God helped these people in spite of their weaknesses, and he will help you as well.

You don't need to be an expert on the Bible or a trained teacher to lead a Bible discussion. The idea behind these inductive studies is that the leader guides group members to discover for themselves what the Bible has to say. This method of learning will allow group members to remember much more of what is said than a lecture would.

These studies are designed to be led easily. As a matter of fact, the flow of questions through the passage from observation to interpretation to application is so natural that you may feel that the studies lead themselves. This study guide is also flexible. You can use it with a variety of groups—student, professional, neighborhood or church groups. Each study takes forty-five to sixty minutes in a group setting.

There are some important facts to know about group dynamics and encouraging discussion. The suggestions listed below should enable you to effectively and enjoyably fulfill your role as leader.

Preparing for the Study

1. Ask God to help you understand and apply the passage in your own life. Unless this happens, you will not be prepared to lead others. Pray too for the various members of the group. Ask God to open your hearts to the message of his Word and motivate you to action.

2. Read the introduction to the entire guide to get an overview of the entire book and the issues which will be explored.

3. As you begin each study, read and reread the assigned Bible passage to familiarize yourself with it.

4. This study guide is based on the New International Version of the Bible. It will help you and the group if you use this translation as the basis for your study and discussion.

5. Carefully work through each question in the study. Spend time in meditation and reflection as you consider how to respond.

6. Write your thoughts and responses in the space provided in the study guide. This will help you to express your understanding of the passage clearly.

7. It might help to have a Bible dictionary handy. Use it to look up any unfamiliar words, names or places. (For additional help on how to study a passage, see chapter five of *How to Lead a LifeBuilder Study*, IVP, 2018.)

8. Consider how you can apply the Scripture to your life. Remember that the group will follow your lead in responding to the studies. They will not go any deeper than you do.

9. Once you have finished your own study of the passage, familiarize yourself with the leader's notes for the study you are leading. These are designed to help you in several ways. First, they tell you the purpose the study guide author had in mind when writing the study. Take time to think through how the study questions work together to accomplish that purpose. Second, the notes provide you with additional background information or suggestions on group dynamics for various questions. This information can be useful when people have difficulty understanding or answering a question. Third, the leader's notes can alert you to potential problems you may encounter during the study.

10. If you wish to remind yourself of anything mentioned in the leader's notes, make a note to yourself below that question in the study.

Leading the Study

1. Begin the study on time. Open with prayer, asking God to help the group to understand and apply the passage.

2. Be sure that everyone in your group has a study guide. Encourage the group to prepare beforehand for each discussion by reading the introduction to the guide and by working through the questions in the study.

3. At the beginning of your first time together, explain that these studies are meant to be discussions, not lectures. Encourage the members of the group to participate. However, do not put pressure on those who may be hesitant to speak during the first few sessions. You may want to suggest the following guidelines to your group.

☐ Stick to the topic being discussed.

☐ Your responses should be based on the verses which are the focus of the discussion and not on outside authorities such as commentaries or speakers.

☐ These studies focus on a particular passage of Scripture. Only rarely should you refer to other portions of the Bible. This allows for everyone to participate in in-depth study on equal ground.

☐ Anything said in the group is considered confidential and will not be discussed outside the group unless specific permission is given to do so.

☐ We will listen attentively to each other and provide time for each person present to talk.

☐ We will pray for each other.

4. Have a group member read the introduction at the beginning of the discussion.

5. Every session begins with a group discussion question. The question or activity is meant to be used before the passage is read. The question introduces the theme of the study and encourages group members to begin to open up. Encourage as many members as possible to participate, and be ready to get the discussion going with your own response.

This section is designed to reveal where our thoughts or feelings need to be transformed by Scripture. That is why it is especially important not to read the passage before the discussion question is asked. The passage will tend to color the honest reactions people would otherwise give because they are, of course, supposed to think the way the Bible does.

You may want to supplement the group discussion question with an icebreaker to help people to get comfortable. See the community section of the *Small Group Starter Kit* (IVP, 1995) for more ideas.

You also might want to use the personal reflection question with your group. Either allow a time of silence for people to respond individually or discuss it together.

6. Have a group member (or members if the passage is long) read aloud the passage to be studied. Then give people several minutes to read the passage again silently so that they can take it all in.

7. Question 1 will generally be an overview question designed to briefly survey the passage. Encourage the group to look at the whole passage, but try to avoid getting sidetracked by questions or issues that will be addressed later in the study.

8. As you ask the questions, keep in mind that they are designed to be used just as they are written. You may simply read them aloud. Or you may prefer to express them in your own words.

There may be times when it is appropriate to deviate from the study guide.

For example, a question may have already been answered. If so, move on to the next question. Or someone may raise an important question not covered in the guide. Take time to discuss it, but try to keep the group from going off on tangents.

9. Avoid answering your own questions. If necessary, repeat or rephrase them until they are clearly understood. Or point out something you read in the leader's notes to clarify the context or meaning. An eager group quickly becomes passive and silent if they think the leader will do most of the talking.

10. Don't be afraid of silence. People may need time to think about the question before formulating their answers.

11. Don't be content with just one answer. Ask, "What do the rest of you think?" or "Anything else?" until several people have given answers to the question.

12. Acknowledge all contributions. Try to be affirming whenever possible. Never reject an answer. If it is clearly off-base, ask, "Which verse led you to that conclusion?" or again, "What do the rest of you think?"

13. Don't expect every answer to be addressed to you, even though this will probably happen at first. As group members become more at ease, they will begin to truly interact with each other. This is one sign of healthy discussion.

14. Don't be afraid of controversy. It can be very stimulating. If you don't resolve an issue completely, don't be frustrated. Move on and keep it in mind for later. A subsequent study may solve the problem.

15. Periodically summarize what the group has said about the passage. This helps to draw together the various ideas mentioned and gives continuity to the study. But don't preach.

16. At the end of the Bible discussion you may want to allow group members a time of quiet to work on an idea under "Now or Later." Then discuss what you experienced. Or you may want to encourage group members to work on these ideas between meetings. Give an opportunity during the session for people to talk about what they are learning.

17. Conclude your time together with conversational prayer, adapting the prayer suggestion at the end of the study to your group. Ask for God's help in following through on the commitments you've made.

18. End on time.

Many more suggestions and helps are found in *How to Lead a LifeBuilder Study.*

Components of Small Groups

A healthy small group should do more than study the Bible. There are four components to consider as you structure your time together.

Nurture. Small groups help us to grow in our knowledge and love of God. Bible study is the key to making this happen and is the foundation of your small group.

Community. Small groups are a great place to develop deep friendships with other Christians. Allow time for informal interaction before and after each study. Plan activities and games that will help you get to know each other. Spend time having fun together—going on a picnic or cooking dinner together.

Worship and prayer. Your study will be enhanced by spending time praising God together in prayer or song. Pray for each other's needs—and keep track of how God is answering prayer in your group. Ask God to help you to apply what you are learning in your study.

Outreach. Reaching out to others can be a practical way of applying what you are learning, and it will keep your group from becoming self-focused. Host a series of evangelistic discussions for your friends or neighbors. Clean up the yard of an elderly friend. Serve at a soup kitchen together, or spend a day working in the community.

Many more suggestions and helps in each of these areas are found in the *Small Group Starter Kit.* You will also find information on building a small group. Reading through the starter kit will be worth your time.

Study 1.
Hosea 1:1—2:13. A Share in God's Pain.

Purpose To identify with the pain God feels for his people when we drift away from him into the world's sinful ways.

Question 1. Since we are shocked and offended by the idea of a prophet marrying an immoral woman at God's command, there have been many attempts to explain and reinterpret Hosea's marriage to Gomer. There are three typical theories: (1) Hosea was told to marry a woman who was already a prostitute; (2) Gomer was pure when Hosea married her but later became immoral; or (3) the "marriage" is only symbolic of God's relationship with Israel, and Hosea never literally married Gomer.

The second interpretation seems to best fit the historical relationship between Israel and the Lord. "If she had been impure at marriage the analogy to Israel would not fit—Israel was pure and became impure, as Gomer had done" (Walter A. Elwell, ed., *Shaw Pocket Bible Handbook* [Wheaton, Ill.: Harold Shaw, 1984], p. 222). In any case it is always dangerous to explain away what the Scriptures say since by doing so we disregard the authority of

God's Word and leave it open to any interpretation. Certainly, in this case it only weakens the impact of Hosea's writing.

Question 2. Let group members respond or not respond as they wish. Let each group member's self-evaluation stand, whether or not you agree with it.

Question 3. While having natural love and protectiveness for his children, Hosea must have wondered if they were truly his, especially in light of the names God gave them: names illustrating unfaithfulness and rebellion.

The story of the massacre at Jezreel (1:4) is related in 2 Kings 9—10. God had commanded Jehu to wipe out the "house" of the wicked king Ahab. "Jehu showed unnecessary cruelty when he slew not only the house of Ahab at Jezreel, but also the visiting monarch from Judah, Ahaziah, and almost all the members of the Davidic family (2 Kings 9:27; 10:13-14). Jehu, further-more, extended this massacre to all the friends of the ruling family (2 Kings 10:11). The point is most evident that divine approval for an act does not thereby carry with it indifference as to how that act is accomplished and how many others it may involve" (Walter C. Kaiser Jr. et al., *Hard Sayings of the Bible* [Downers Grove, Ill.: InterVarsity Press, 1996], p. 236).

Question 4. Use this question to emphasize how sin violates God's exclusive claim on our love and reverence and how it contaminates our loving response to God.

Question 5. Think of specific situations when you have needed to show both justice and mercy. For example, your teenager came home several hours past her curfew with a questionable excuse.

Question 6. While the passage is full of God's judgment, verses 1:10-11 reveal that God will not give up on his people.

Question 8. It is interesting to note the uses of the word *therefore* in this passage (2:6, 9; see also 2:14). God's purpose was to persuade Israel, the people he loved, that they needed him. His methods seem harsh, but his purposes were for their ultimate good and for the sake of their relationship with him. He longed to bring Israel back to himself.

Question 9. When Israel was about to enter Canaan after their slavery in Egypt, God promised them that they would prosper if they obeyed him; he also warned that they would face disaster if they disobeyed him (Deut 28). The threats of 2:9-13 are only a fulfillment of God's historic warnings.

Question 10. This is a personal question. People should be given an opportunity to respond if they wish, but don't press for a response. Point out how, when we love a wayward person, we share a little of God's pain over that person.

Question 11. This question may surprise group members because it takes the study in an unexpected turn. The Bible not only shows us the condition of humanity in general; it shows us our own shortcomings. James 1:22-25 likens the Word of God to a mirror that tells us the truth about ourselves.

Study 2. Hosea 2:14—3:5. A Vision of the Possible.

Purpose: To explore God's hope for his people despite their present wanderings.

Question 3. God longed for Israel to be intimate with him, to forsake their rival gods, to be faithful to him and to love him.

Question 4. Notice the action verbs ("I will") that are ascribed to God.

Question 5. God will respond favorably to Jezreel, and the other two names have been reversed: "Not my loved one" will be loved by God, and "not my people" will be called the people of God. God's mercy has changed everything.

Question 6. It is not clear why or from whom Hosea had to buy Gomer back. There is evidence that the price he paid was the market value of a slave. Therefore, Gomer may have sunk to the point of selling herself into slavery, or she may have gotten into a debt she could not possibly repay. Verse 3:3 is the first time the NIV uses the word *prostitute* in relation to Gomer, though other translations refer to her "harlotry" from the beginning of the book. The word could refer either to a common prostitute or to a cult prostitute of Baal's fertility rites.

The prediction of the Israelites living many days without religious or secular leadership (3:4) apparently refers to their coming exile into Assyria. More will be said about this in study 8.

Question 8. Hosea would have to give up any pride, resentment, unforgiveness, grudges and self-righteousness.

Questions 9-11. These are personal questions. Be ready to give your own responses to encourage group members that it is safe to be open about their failures.

Study 3. Hosea 4. Back to the Present.

Purpose: To examine how unfaithfulness to God brings destruction to a society.

Question 1. Verse 1 provides the reason that Israelite society had become corrupt: there was "no faithfulness, no love, no acknowledgment of God in the land."

Gilgal (v. 15) was the site of the first shrine built to the Lord in Canaan, immediately after Israel crossed the Jordan River. There Joshua set up stones as a memorial to what God had done (Josh 4:19-24). Ironically, Gilgal had been degraded to a place for sin, as Amos also pointed out (Amos 4:4).

Beth Aven (v. 15), "house of idolatry," refers to Bethel, which means "house of God" but was a city where Jeroboam had set up a golden calf idol.

Note how in Hosea's time, as now, human sin and selfishness reap consequences in the natural world (v. 3).

Question 3. As we read verses 10-14, the word *prostitution* keeps hitting us between the eyes. Because the references are tied to idol worship, it appears that Israelite women engaged in religious prostitution in or near temples devoted to Canaanite fertility gods.

This religion was predicated upon the belief that the processes of nature were controlled by the relations between gods and goddesses. Projecting their understanding of their own sexual activities, the worshipers of these deities, through the use of imitative magic, engaged in sexual intercourse with devotees of the shrine, in the belief that this would encourage the gods and goddesses to do likewise. Only by sexual relations among the deities could man's desire for increase in herds and fields, as well as in his own family, be realized. (O. J. Baab, "Prostitution," in *The Interpreter's Dictionary of the Bible*, ed. George A. Buttrick [Nashville: Abingdon, 1962], 3:932-33)

The sacrifices offered in Canaanite temples resembled those which the Israelites offered to Yahweh, the God of Israel, in the names of the sacrifices and the beasts offered as well as in the ritual observed. But the religion was polytheistic and highly sensuous, with a strong emphasis on fertility rites. In the temples of the Canaanites there were male and female prostitutes ("sacred" men and women), and all sorts of sexual excesses were practiced. It was believed that in some way these rites caused the crops and the herds to prosper. Baal was the god who cared for the rain and the growth of the crops and the flocks. (J. A. Thompson, *The Bible and Archaeology* [Grand Rapids, Mich.: Eerdmans, 1982], p. 90)

Question 4. When the Israelites sold themselves to the Canaanite god Baal, they took the reverence that rightly belonged to God and threw it away on an idol.

Question 5. Gomer's sinful life vividly illustrates how the Israelites sold themselves away from the Lord.

Question 7. The gain does not have to be financial. We may compromise our faith in order to gain or keep social status, to avoid risk, to stay comfortable or to insulate ourselves from rejection.

Question 10. God could not reward Israel while they were set on idolatry; it would have only affirmed and encouraged their idolatry since they attributed their prosperity to Baal. Yet it is clear that God *wanted* to "pasture them like lambs in a meadow." (For another example of how Israel's sin restricted God's blessings, look back to Hosea 2:8-9.)

Study 4. Hosea 5. Sins of the Leadership.

Purpose: To consider how ungodly leadership, whether secular or religious, draws people away from God.

General note. "Hosea begins chapter 5 with a threefold summons for judgment to three groups: priests, house of Israel, and house of the king. Though the house of Israel probably refers to all the people, it is likely that the tribe chieftains of the northern kingdom are the target along with the priests and the kings and royal court" (Lloyd J. Ogilvie, *The Communicator's Commentary* [Dallas: Word, 1990], 20:88).

Verse 3 introduces the name "Ephraim," which will be prominent throughout the rest of the book of Hosea. Ephraim, one of the sons of Joseph, is used as another name for the northern kingdom of Israel. Though the southern kingdom of Judah is mentioned in Hosea's prophecies, Ephraim (Israel) is his main target.

Question 2. If we discount the idea that God was just spouting off (why would he need to?), we must conclude that God was going to tremendous lengths to warn the people that idolatry had terrible consequences, in the hope that they would see the truth and renounce their idols. As God sent Hosea to seek out Gomer and redeem her (chapter 3), God longed to bring his beloved people back to himself.

Question 3. "The very familiar image of fowlers trapping birds in nets and snares may be the origin of this common metaphor (see Josh 23:13; Ps 69:22; Is 8:14)" (John H. Walton, Victor H. Matthews and Mark W. Chavalas, *The IVP Bible Background Commentary: Old Testament* [Downers Grove, Ill.: InterVarsity Press, 2000], p. 755).

Questions 4-5. Notice how the "spirit of prostitution" was still in Israel's heart (v. 4); they hoped that God could be found within their Baal worship. As long as people seek spirituality in a god of their own making, trying to create a "user-friendly" god who does what they want, the God of the Bible will be repulsive to them.

Question 6. "Gibeah and Ramah were both high among the mountains of central Palestine. The sound of alarm from these eminences could be heard in both Judah and Israel. . . . Judah is pictured as awaiting the overthrow of Israel, after which she could cross the frontier and appropriate Israelite territory" (Charles F. Pfeiffer, "Hosea," in *Wycliffe Bible Commentary* [Nashville: Southwestern, 1962], p. 807).

The moving of boundary stones (v. 10) was forbidden by God's law (Deut 19:14). "Since the land had been given to the people by God and apportioned according to a God-given formula, to move boundary stones and thus appropriate territory unlawfully was a crime of theft against God" (Walton, Matthews and Chavalas, *IVP Bible Background Commentary*, p. 192).

Question 8. The reference is probably to King Menahem's payoff to Pul, king of Assyria (2 Kings 15:19-20). The deal worked—temporarily.

Study 5. Hosea 6:1-10. A Temporary Repentance.

Purpose: To affirm that repentance means a change of heart rather than correct words or the proper form of worship.

Questions 2-3. Israel's hopes are full of nature imagery: the rising sun, the refreshing rains. To a sincere seeker, the Lord will appear in those ways and more. Yet God saw that their love for him was as ephemeral as mist and dew. The people's motive for supposedly returning to God (to gain his short-term blessings) is identical with their motive for turning to idols.

Question 5. When Jesus was challenged by self-righteous faultfinders, he quoted part of verse 6 (Mt 9:13; 12:7).

Question 6. "What was the use of piling on sacrifices if they were not expressions of a spirit of contrition and genuine piety of life? God always inspects the giver, even in the Old Testament, before he inspects the gift, offering or praise. How can one who is unclean offer a clean sacrifice?" (Kaiser, *Hard Sayings*, p. 275).

Question 7. A sacrifice or offering, no matter how expensive, can be made without any repentance from the heart. To put money in a collection plate or lay something on the altar is a purely external act. An observer can discern nothing about the giver's spiritual condition. Mercy (or "steadfast love") and the acknowledgment (or "knowledge") of God are inward qualities which inevitably show on the outside.

Study 6. Hosea 6:11—7:16. No Place to Hide.

Purpose: To determine to be honest with the Lord and with ourselves.

Question 1. The diverse images share the qualities of instability and unreliability. The images of heat show the intensity of Israel's pursuit of wickedness.

The oven depicted here was made of clay and was cylindrical in shape. . . . It may have been embedded into the floor or lay on it. The domed roof had a large hole covered by a door through which the baker would first add fuel (wood, dried grass, dung or cakes made from olive residue). Flames would escape through the hole until a hot bed of coals remained. The heat would be captured as the door was closed and would remain for many hours (enough for the bread to be kneaded and allowed to rise). Then the baker would place the slightly raised flat bread on the inner walls of the oven or amongst the coals. The metaphor plays on these mundane tasks and well-known images. (Walton, Matthews and Chavalas, *IVP Bible Background Commentary*, p. 756)

As a nation Israel was literally "half-baked!"

The imagery abruptly changes from a baker's oven to a not very bright bird that flits back and forth in indecision. "Clearly, Israel's kings have been snared in the net of political ambitions cast by both of the ancient super powers, Egypt and Assyria" (Walton, Matthews and Chavalas, *IVP Bible Background Commentary*, p. 756).

Finally, God compares Israel to a bow that is likely to break in the archer's hands. "The composite bow, made from a combination of wood, horn and animal tendons, . . . was subject to changes in weather and humidity. If it was not kept in a case, it could lose its strength and be described as unreliable or slack (see Ps 78:57)" (Walton, Matthews and Chavalas, *IVP Bible Background Commentary*, p. 756).

Questions 7-8. To heal, redeem, train and strengthen are the desires of one who has at heart only what is best of the one being helped. There is no hint of revenge or vindictiveness by God toward his people.

Question 11. Since our attempts to deceive the Lord also involve self-deception, answers may not spring to mind either for your group members or for yourself. This question deserves further thought and prayer throughout the week.

Study 7. Hosea 8:1—9:9. Substitute Gods.

Purpose: To contrast idolatry with true worship of God.

Question 1. Note especially the Lord's condemnation of a calf-idol (8:5-6). "The calf could mean a calf idol in the city of Samaria or the royal sanctuary at Bethel. Jeroboam I erected calf images at Bethel and identified them not only as gods but confused them with Yahweh" (Ogilvie, *Communicator's Commentary*, p. 122). First Kings 12:26-33 tells how Jeroboam I set up his own idols and system of worship to rival Jerusalem; we know from 2 Kings 10:28-29 that the images were still standing not long before Hosea's time.

Question 3. The Israelites had altars, they made sacrifices, and they knew God's law. Verses 8:11-13 give God's response to Israel's self-congratulation.

Question 5. Idols may be material things, people, ambitions, causes or anything else that takes the place of God. Consider both the things people depend on daily and the things they depend on in crisis.

Question 10. God called the prophet a watchman over Ephraim. The people saw him as out of touch with reality and even dangerous. The prophet deserved honor but drew hostility. "Hosea's enemies attempt to discredit him by claiming his prophecies are actually just the ravings of a madman (compare the similar charges made in Amos 7:10 and Jer 29:25-28)" (Walton, Matthews and Chavalas, *IVP Bible Background Commentary*, p. 757).

Questions 12-13. "There is too often a real difference between the God we worship and the gods we serve. But the gods we serve are those in which we really believe, for they direct the course of our lives and by them we pattern our conduct. The most cursory examination of our lives will show that the goals for which we strive are vastly more in keeping with 'the God of this world' than with the God and Father of our Lord Jesus Christ. We worship the God of Jesus; but we serve our own gods. This too is a form of idolatry" (Harold Cooke Phillips, "The Book of Hosea," in *The Interpreter's Bible*, ed. George A. Buttrick [New York: Abingdon, 1956], 6:647).

Study 8. Hosea 9:10—10:15. Recalling Young Love.

Purpose: To trace the decline in Israel's love for God since he chose them and began his relationship with them.

Question 2. "There is a sense of unexpected pleasure to be found in grapes growing in the desert or ripe figs in the early part of the summer. . . . They are considered such a delicacy that they are to be eaten immediately after picking (see Is 28:4; Nahum 3:12)" (Walton, Matthews, and Chavalas, *IVP Bible Background Commentary*, p. 757). The vine is used other places in Scripture as a metaphor for Israel (for example, Ps 80).

The incident at Baal Peor (9:10) came during Israel's wanderings after they left Egypt (Num 25). It was not their first fall into idolatry after the exodus. Aaron set up a gold calf idol even while Moses was receiving God's law on Mt. Sinai (Ex 32). The Moabite idol at Baal Peor, like the Canaanite religion, was specifically connected with sexual immorality.

Question 5. Israel would be taken into exile in Assyria, and Samaria and its king would vanish. Second Kings 17:1-17 tells how Shalmaneser, king of Assyria, attacked Israel during the reign of its last king, Hoshea. Shalmaneser deported the Israelites and imported his own people. The Bible is clear that this happened because of Israel's idolatry.

Question 7. "It may be that young oxen were first trained to accept the yoke by putting them to work on the threshing floor. This relatively simple task, during which they had the opportunity of the reward of grazing (Deut 25:4), made them more docile (see Jer 50:11). Once they had achieved the stage when direction was easy, then a sledge could be added that would get the animals used to pulling a load (2 Sam 24:22). This in turn prepared them for the more disciplined task of plowing a furrow in a virgin field (1 Kings 19:19; Jer 4:3). In like manner, God chooses to use the docile and strong Israel to fulfill the divine plan" (Walton, Matthews, and Chavalas, *IVP Bible Background Commentary*, p. 758).

Question 11. Israel trusted in their own strength instead of in the Lord. Like all humanity through the ages, they met the question "Who is God?" with the answer "We are!" Self-reliance rather than God-reliance has been at the heart of sin ever since Adam and Eve decided to take things into their own hands rather than to obey God.

Study 9. Hosea 11:1-11. Mercy Overrules.

Purpose: To reflect on the mercy of God to Israel and to us.

Questions 1-2. In this passage God speaks some of the tenderest "human" language in the book of Hosea and, indeed, in the entire Bible. The images reveal the depth of God's love for humanity just as surely as the preceding images reveal his righteous judgment.

Question 7. "The cry is heart-rending. God had loved his people, yet justice demanded that they be punished. Since God could not lightly forget the earlier days of Israel's faithfulness, he decreed judgment with great reluctance. Admah . . . Zeboiim were cities of the plain which were overthrown with Sodom and Gomorrah (Gen. 19). . . . Although judgment would fall upon Israel, in wrath God would remember mercy. Israel was not to be forever cast off, although she would be sorely chastised" (Pfeiffer, "Hosea," p. 814).

Questions 9-10. If you have ever gotten into a discussion about hell, you have probably heard God's love maligned as inferior to human love. The argument goes like this: any human parent will forgive and take back a child unconditionally, so how can God bear to see anyone lost? This Scripture turns the tables and reveals the egotism of that argument. Ultimately, all human love is fickle and imperfect; only the character of God is constant and unchanging. Walt Kaiser writes, "The sudden shift in Hosea 11:8-9 signals new hope for Israel. The main reasons for the shift from a message of judgment to one of hope are to be found in two facts: (1) Israel would suffer a full punishment for disloyalty and would go into exile under the Assyrian conquest, and (2) the character of God, like the faces of a coin, has two sides: judgment and compassion.

"In the freedom of God, he chose to deal with Israel after its exile under his attribute of grace and compassion" (Kaiser et al., *Hard Sayings*, p. 324).

Study 10. Hosea 11:12—12:14. Yet Justice Prevails.

Purpose: To be confronted by the justice of God and to resolve to be just.

Question 1. Jacob's life is related in detail in Genesis 25—49. The account of his birth (12:3) is told in Genesis 25:21-26; his struggle with the angel of the Lord (12:3-4) is in Genesis 32:22-32; his vision at Bethel (12:4) is in Genesis 28:10-22; and his service for a wife (12:12) is in Genesis 29.

Question 2. The people of Israel, Jacob's descendants, were repeating Jacob's personal history as they fluctuated between devotion and deviousness.

Question 3. Take a long or short time with this question depending on how much your group members already know about Jacob's life. Be careful not to get sidetracked into a study of his entire history.

Question 5. It will help to think of examples from both personal life (such as dealing with family members or work situations) and national life (such as government policy toward the poor).

Question 9. Verse 12:11 may refer to the destruction of Gilead by Tiglath-Pileser in 2 Kings 15:29 because of idol worship. The surrounding verses refer to God's consistent faithfulness and deliverance.

Study 11. Hosea 13. The Sign of Love.

Purpose: To see God's discipline as evidence of his love.

Question 1. Note especially verses 4-6 and verses 9-11. Israel declined into pride after God had delivered them from Egypt and made them prosper in Canaan. God had warned them of such a decline (Deut 8:10-20).

Question 3. If this question seems too abstract, identify some idols which control people's lives today. Consider how devotion to each one "kills" the worshiper because it negates the worshiper's life as it was meant to be lived. In some cases the idol could even bring physical death (such as drugs, inordinate risk-taking, crime), but more typically the idol deals death to the worshiper's spirit.

Throughout the book of Hosea, you have read about the spiritual death of Israel—separation from their God—even while they lived in apparent power and prosperity. Eventually they were taken into captivity from which they never returned (Judah returned but not Israel).

Question 5. Assyria would be the instrument of the Lord's wrath, but the Lord would be the actual attacker. Second Kings 17 tells the story of Assyria's conquest of the northern kingdom of Israel, along with a lengthy explanation of why God allowed it to happen.

Question 6. The Lord's purpose is that Israel—and all people—will acknowledge him as the only God. This is the first commandment: "You shall have no other gods before me" (Ex 20:3).

Question 7. God wills life for his people, and therefore, he disciplines in unpleasant ways. Hebrews 12:4-13 is a New Testament statement of the same principle.

Question 9. Human pride makes it difficult for people to accept help from the one they are rebelling against, and the help is unlikely to fulfill the desires that caused the rebellion in the first place.

Study 12. Hosea 14. God's Final Promise.

Purpose To commit ourselves to the Lord wholeheartedly because he is trustworthy.

Question 1. After thirteen chapters of alternating judgment and mercy, the prophecy of Hosea ends with a lavish vision of a great future where God and Israel are completely reconciled. There is a finality about Hosea's vision, as though nothing could ever spoil it again.

Question 3. Some possibilities: good deeds, busyness in Christian service, perfect attendance at worship or Bible study, respectable appearance, money, time.

Questions 4-5. As we have seen throughout Hosea, this passage is full of rich images. Here they practically burst with healthy, flourishing life. All these visions of prosperity and security are the results of God's care rather than the fruit of Israel's own efforts.

Questions 7-8. God's lavish promises are not meant to excuse sin. He still wants Israel to repent of their idolatry and worship him alone. Because he is just, he cannot ignore sin. Because he is merciful, he will forgive Israel when they turn back to him.

Prayer. Give group members the opportunity to read their prayers aloud if they wish. Close this final session with a time of silence in which all members read their written prayers to themselves. Then end with spoken prayer for the group.

Dale and Sandy Larsen are freelance writers living in Rochester, Minnesota. They have written more than forty books and Bible study guides, including the LifeBuilder Bible Studies Faith: Depending on God, Questions God Asks *and* Couples of the Old Testament.